Once I Was A Child And There Was Much Pain...

Once I Was a Child And There Was Much Pain...

a glimpse into the soul
of an incest survivor

by
Nancy E. Strout

OTIS PUBLISHING
341 Spurwink Avenue
Cape Elizabeth, Maine 04107

Second Edition

PRINTED IN THE UNITED STATES OF AMERICA

Library of Congress Cataloging in Publication Data

Strout, Nancy, E. 1956 -
    Once I was a child and there was much pain . . .: a glimpse into the soul of an incest survivor / by Nancy E. Strout - - 1st ed.
      p. cm.
   ISBN 1-4923634-4-8 : $6.95
    1. Strout, Nancy, E. 1956—Pictorial works. 2. Adult child abuse victims–United States–Pictorial works. I. Title.
RC569.5.C55E37 1988
616.85'83–dc19
                                                       88-28281
                                                          CIP

For Peter, Zach, Meg, Ben and Ryan

who have traveled through the darkness with me.

Thanks to:

Henry Giaretto, Ph.D. for his encouragement; the Leader of my A.M.A.C. group Marsha Baker, M.A., with whom my journey began, Nancy Dix, M.S.W. for her guidance in my early days of therapy, and Parents United for their interest in my project.

I was a child once and there was much pain.

I am a woman now and I speak of that pain thru my art.

Here within these covers I share it with you.

OH DADDY!....NO

THE SCREAM WITHIN IS

DEEP

AND

SILENT

I AM BAD

NANCY E.

OH ISN'T SHE PRETTY!
WOULD YOU LIKE TO USE HER?

Nancy E.

I AM NOT SEEN

I AM NOT HEARD

ALL IS TORMENT

NANCYE

WHERE ARE THE FACES

NANCY E.

THE DREAM

I AM ALONE

THE ROOM IS BOARDED

WINDOW AND DOOR

THERE IS NO ESCAPE

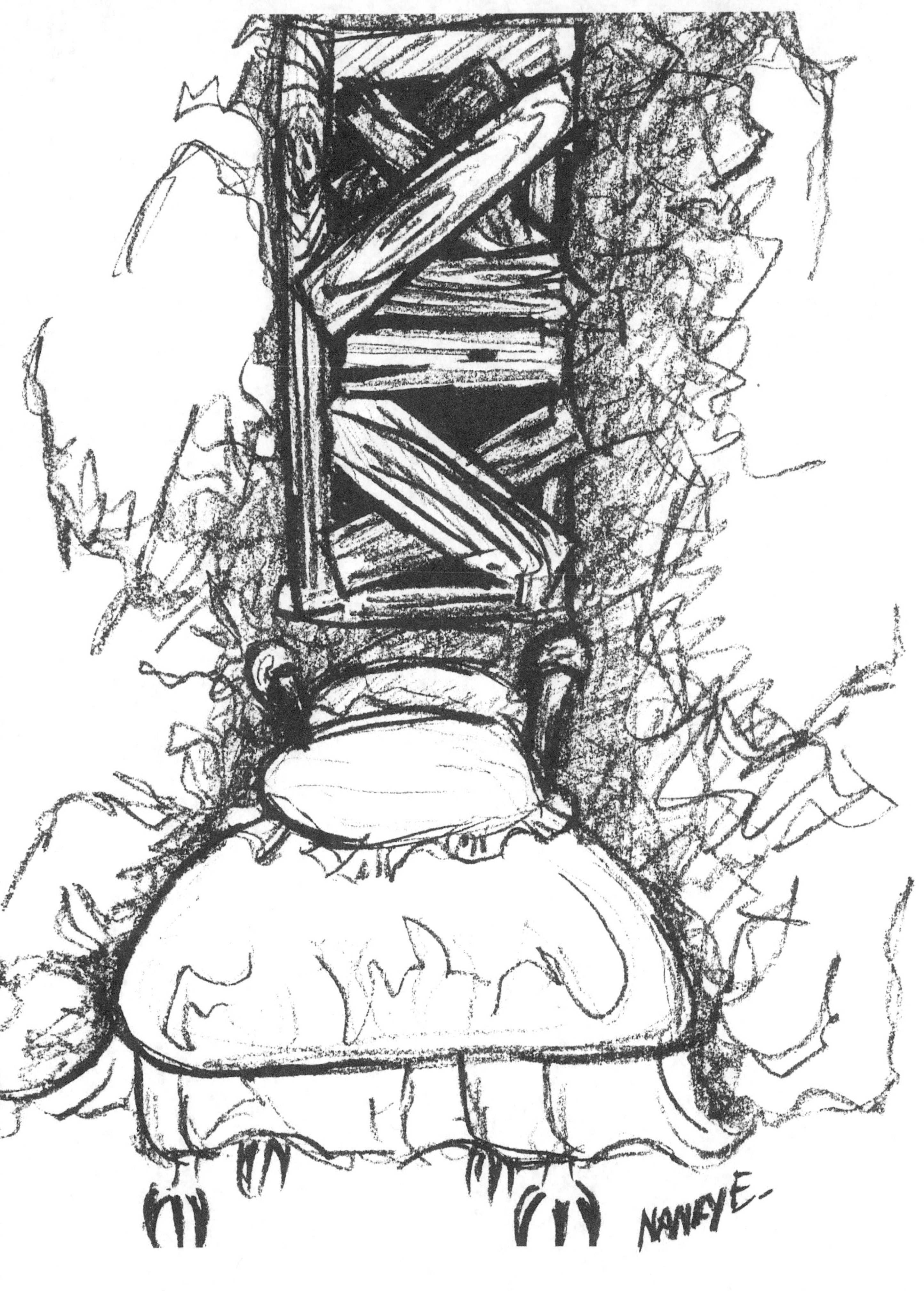

NOT A DREAM

IMPRISONED

A FARM VACATION
NANCY E.

I AM HURT

I AM TORN

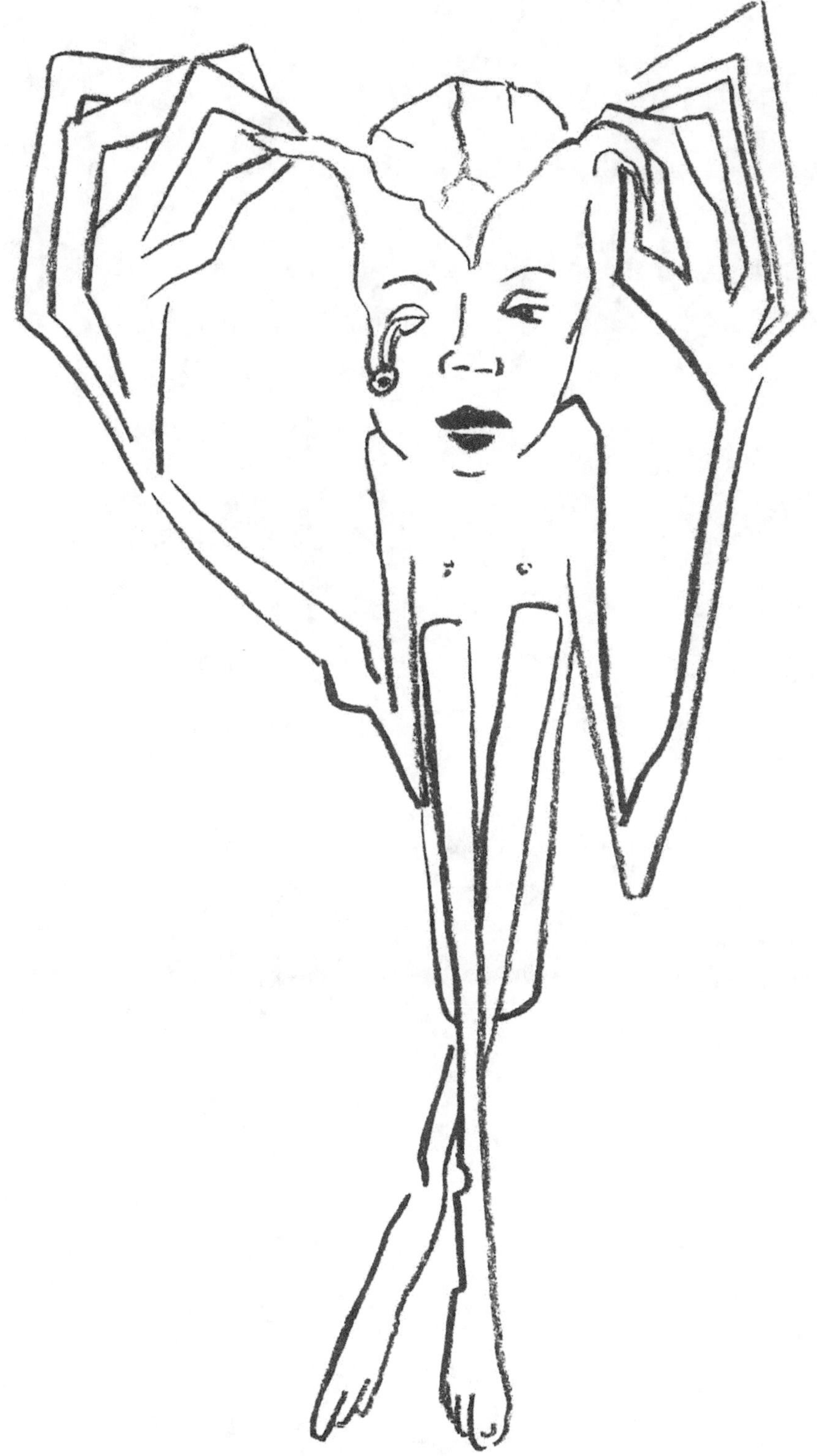

Nancye.

WE MUSTN'T SEE THIS

WHY DO WE

SEE

THIS!

NANCYE

ANOTHER DREAM

MY COAT IS STRONG AND WARM

I KNOW NOT OF THE KEY

NANCY E.

THE IDEA OF DEATH WAS GOOD

I AM BREAKING INTO PIECES

NANCYE.

EVIL IN ALL ITS FORMS THREATENS

TO

ENGULF

ME

NANCY E.

I AM
THE FAMILY TOY

WATCHED

USED

LEFT

NANCYE

BORN FEMALE
USED CHILD
TORMENTED CREATURE

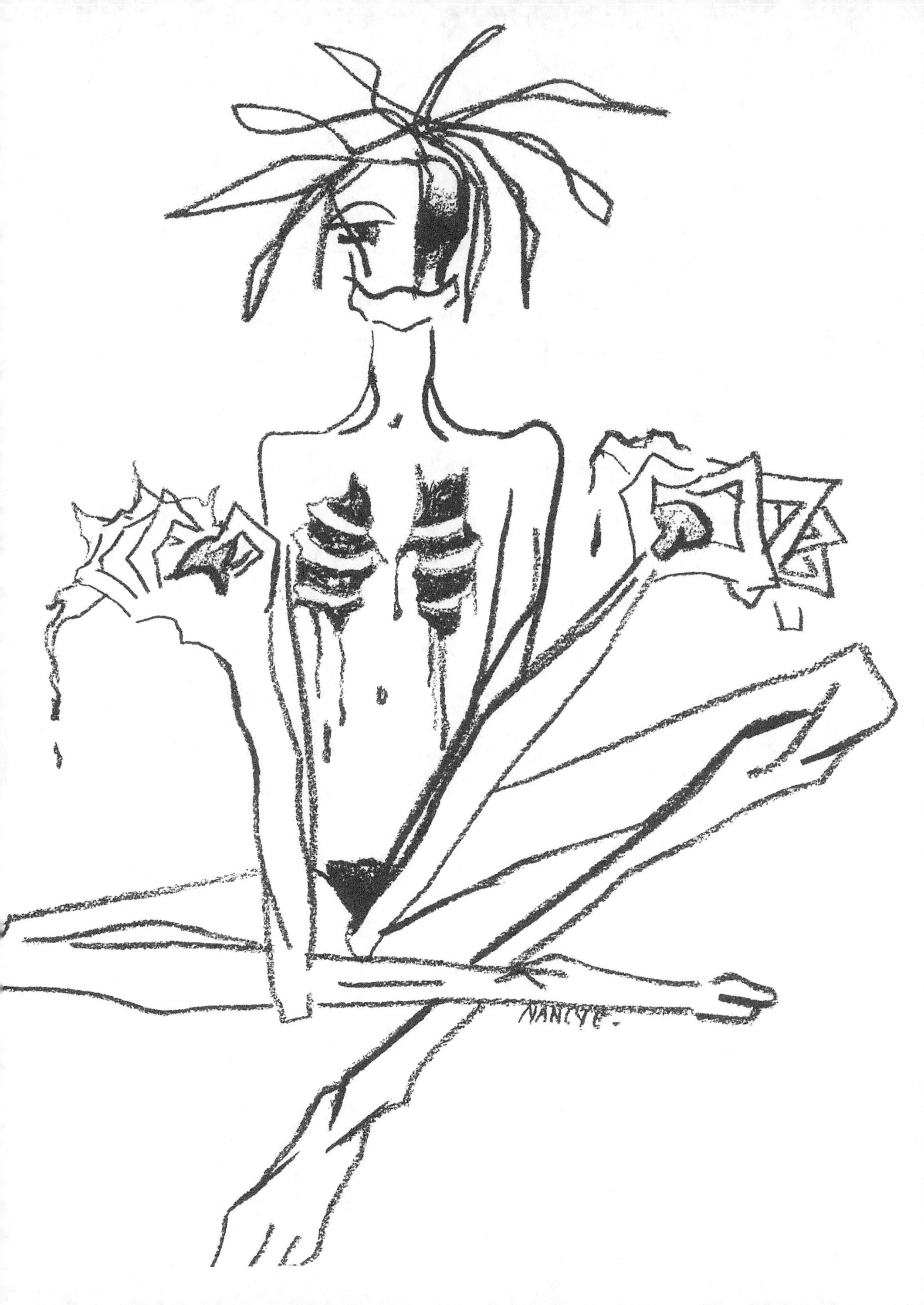
NANCYE.

I DRAW ALL THAT I AM

NANCYE-

INSECURE HIDE AWAY

Nancy E.

I *KNOW* THEY ARE THERE

Nancy is a "beautiful child" of twenty-eight working very hard to catch-up emotionally. A talented artist and a bright and searching student at an eastern university, she's also a wife and mother of four children.

Her course in therapy is long and arduous as she struggles to understand the impact her childhood has had on her life. She works at breaking through the maladaptive coping mechanisms she once needed to survive.

As exemplified in her last drawing where through the very small window the sun shines, rainbows stretch before small birds and the world is in light, Nancy knows there is beauty. Intellectually she tastes it occasionally yet emotionally she is unable to leave her dark corner.

Nancy uses her art to express the feelings that still live in her dark space and to learn to go beyond those haunting fears to a better place where she can feel free to trust and love.

Nancy's Therapist
M.J.A.

www.ingramcontent.com/pod-product-compliance
Lightning Source LLC
Chambersburg PA
CBHW081237250726
48654CB00012B/1367